LUNCH IN A JAR

30 quick, easy and nourishing lunchtime recipes that will have you munching your way through your 5 a day

By Fiona Manning

www.earthinspired.co.uk

Cover Design by John Foscolos

Photography by Jim Thirion

Edited by Dawn Jackson Williams

Copyright 2016 Fiona Manning.

All rights reserved.

Please do not reproduce material without prior permission from the author.

Table of Contents

Acknowledgements — 8

Introduction — 9

What is a lunch in a jar? — 9

Layering a jar — 10

How to use this book — 11

Quick kitchen conversions — 12

About the author — 12

Chapter 1 Sub-Recipes — 13

1. *Blanched vegetables* — *14*
2. *Roasted nuts* — *14*
3. *Spiced roasted pumpkin* — *15*
4. *Grilled peppers and courgette* — *15*
5. *Roasted and toasted pumpkin seeds* — *16*
6. *Roasted beetroot* — *16*
7. *Dry frying and grinding seeds* — *17*

Chapter 2 Vegetarian and Vegan Lunch Pots — 18

8. *Blue cheese, pear and hazelnut salad pot* — *19*
9. *Spiced roasted pumpkin and goat's cheese salad pot* — *20*
10. *Roasted beetroot, goat's cheese and walnut salad pot* — *21*
11. *Potato, garden pea and chive salad pot with lemon butter dressing* — *22*
12. *Roasted root vegetable, feta and toasted pine nut salad pot* — *23*
13. *Asian slaw and ginger, peanut salad dressing salad pot* — *24*
14. *Thai mango and roasted cashew nut salad pot* — *25*
15. *Roasted red pepper, feta and pine nut salad pot* — *26*
16. *Spicy Mexican bean salad pot* — *27*
17. *Grape, avocado and goat's cheese salad pot* — *28*
18. *Greek salad pot* — *29*
19. *Curried roasted vegetable, chickpea, mint and feta salad pot* — *30*
20. *Red lentil and coconut curry pot* — *31*
21. *Sweet potato and chickpea curry pot* — *32*

Chapter 3 Fish Lunch Pots — 33

22. *Orange and thyme poached salmon and endive salad pot* — *34*
23. *Seared tuna steak, sun dried tomato, sweet corn and walnut salad pot* — *35*
24. *Thai spiced salmon salad pot* — *36*
25. *Tuna, tarragon and butterbean salad pot* — *37*
26. *Curry spiced salmon, celery and grape salad pot* — *38*

Chapter 4 Chicken Lunch Pots — 39

27. Spicy chicken, mango and grape salad pot — 40
28. Nutty turmeric chicken salad pot — 41
29. Colourful chicken satay salad pot — 42
30. Balsamic roasted peach, chicken and goat's cheese salad pot — 43
31. Chicken and cashew nut Massaman curry pot — 44
32. Moroccan chicken, apricot and almond stew pot — 45
33. Lebanese chicken salad pot — 46

Chapter 5 Meat Lunch Pots — 47

34. Duck, blueberry and basil salad pot — 48
35. Thai beef salad pot — 49
36. Bacon and egg salad pot with oven roasted asparagus and button mushrooms — 50
37. Mixed pea, mint, feta and bacon salad pot — 51

Conclusion — 52

Index — 53

Acknowledgements

This cookbook would have not been possible without the help of a few key players. So I want to give an enormous thank you to the following people:

Jim Thirion, who dedicated his time and talent to this project by photographing all the Jars. Thank you for your outstanding work.

My mother, Kim Furmston, for her ongoing support throughout this project and for helping me retest and taste test all the recipes. Thank you for always believing in me.

My father, Richard Manning, and his partner Jane Long for helping out with the tasting sessions. Thank you dad for your continuous love and support. I hope this cookbook makes you proud.

My brother, Alex Manning and his girlfriend, Therese Barkhuysen, for fully supporting me throughout this project and keeping me focused. Thank you for your help with recipe development and taste testing.

My sister, Abigail Manning, for her loving encouragement and support, and for her involvement and feedback during the taste testing sessions. Thank you for all your help.

Georgia Allen, for flying me out to Thailand to get this project finished and published. Thank you for believing in me, keeping me focused and for your endless words of encouragement.

John Foscolos for all his help with designing the front cover and working on the photos. Thank you.

Dawn Jackson Williams for her fantastic and professional approach to editing this cookbook.

Introduction

We all get tired, stressed and worn out, and finding the motivation to make lunch for the week is the last thing on our minds. Yet we know how beneficial it would be to our health to swap those empty calories of a quick and easy sandwich for nutrient dense alternatives.

In this book you will learn how to up your daily intake of fruit and vegetables through simple assembly recipes. You will learn a variety of ways of preparing and seasoning your vegetables to make them more exciting. You will replace a portion of carbohydrates or protein with vegetables to bulk out your lunches and to ensure you still feel full. This will naturally reduce the calorie count of the meal whilst increasing the vitamin, nutrient and fiber intake.

This is not a diet book; this is a cookbook for optimal health focusing on the benefits of incorporating more fruit and vegetables into our daily diet. Saying that, vegetables are so low in calories that it is very difficult to gain weight even if you overeat them, so if your aim is to lose weight then you may naturally do so. But I wrote this book not to encourage weight loss but because I feel we can lead healthier lives just by making a few simple adjustments to our lifestyle: one of them being eating a little more of the right stuff and a little less of the bad stuff.

This cookbook is for beginners and experienced cooks alike. It has been designed with sub-recipes explaining certain cooking methods in more detail. So, if you are already an accomplished chef you can skip straight to the recipe without having to go over steps you are already familiar with, and for those of you who are just starting out the recipes are broken down into easy chunks so that you can follow the recipes smoothly.

Finally, this cookbook has been written for all of you who want a quick reference guide for easy-to-make recipes that you can fit into your daily schedule easily and effortlessly.

What is a lunch in a jar?

A lunch in a jar is a convenient, healthy, time friendly way of getting better nutrition into your bodies. All of the recipes in this book have been designed to fit into a Mason jar – of the type with a screw-top lid that you will find in all cookery stores and even in larger supermarkets these days!

There are a number of benefits of using Mason jars to prepare and store your lunches in ahead of time:

1. They will keep your salads fresher for longer.
2. Hot lunches can be prepared in advance as Mason jars are safe to reheat in an oven or microwave (as long as you remove the lid first).
3. You can store the dressing in the same container as the salad, so it's

conveniently all in one.
4. You can also choose to freeze certain recipes in the jar if you prefer to make a larger batch to last a while (freezing is only suitable for the curries and stews).

This makes them extremely versatile and great for storing a variety of meals. This cookbook will give you some inspiration for different hot and cold meals to make in your Mason jars to keep your lunch-times varied, exciting and fun.

All the recipes have been designed to make 1 serving so you can choose to sample just one or multiply the recipe to make enough to suit your needs. Jars will last for up to 5 days in your fridge (see below for salads avocado*) allowing you to prepare your food before mid-week madness sets in.

All the recipes in this book have been made to fit into a 600ml (20 fl oz) mason jar. If you do not have one of these jars to hand you may choose to use another container, that's fine. Just remember though, that they may not keep as well as in a Mason jar and the salad dressing may need to be stored separately (miniature jam pots are good for this). Mason jars are cheaply available online at Amazon and it is always good to have a few to hand if you want to double up on recipes.

* Avocados although full of heart-healthy mono and polyunsaturated fats and essential nutrients they do tend to oxidize quickly, turning brown in a couple of hours. To prevent this you can either choose to brush the avocado with a little bit of lemon juice (the salad will keep for 1-2 days); or keep the avocado out until the morning you intend on eating the salad and pop it in then.

Layering a jar

The key to a successful 'lunch in a jar' is in getting the order of the ingredients right, as this will keep your jar fresher and tastier for longer. There are of course exceptions to the rules, and some of the lunch jars are all in one mixes. Below, however, is a list of the general principles to keep in mind when putting together your lunch in a jar:

1. The dressing is always made first and in the bottom of the jar. By putting the dressing in first rather than at the end you avoid the rest of the ingredients becoming soggy. When ready to eat just turn your jar upside down a couple of times to mix the dressing in.
2. Next to go in is anything that needs marinating. If using fish, chicken or meat it usually goes in at this stage. For the vegetarian dishes anything that is happy to be pickled goes in first: radishes, cucumber, carrots, broccoli etc.
3. The more delicate vegetables and fruit and those which are not so happy being pickled go in next: mushrooms, green beans, courgette, sweet corn, pear, blueberries etc. It is not too detrimental to the salad if these fruit and vegetables are exposed to the dressing but you want to keep in mind that

you don't want your heavier ingredients flattening the more delicate ones.
4. Any cheese going into your jar wants to go it at this stage. Many cheeses are soft or crumbly, so are kept more intact when added at this stage of the salad assembly.
5. Finally any lettuce, nuts or seeds go in last. You want your nuts to retain their crunchiness and you do not want your lettuce getting squashed and going soggy.

How to use this book

The first chapter of this cookbook includes the preparation methods for various vegetables, nuts, seeds and spices. These are the sub-recipes to help make the main recipe section easier to follow. These can also be used independently as side dishes to accompany your meals.

Timings for the sub-recipes are included in the prep and cooking times of the recipes.

All the recipes are gluten and grain free. Symbols for common allergies have been included with each recipe for easy reference. Please follow this list of color-coded symbols:

Gf - Gluten Free
Ef - Egg Free
V - Vegetarian
Vg - Vegan
Sf - Soy Free
Gf - Grain Free
Df - Dairy Free
Nf - Nut Free

Most of the vegetarian recipes can be made vegan, depending on the recipe, by:

- ✓ Substituting the honey for maple syrup
- ✓ Omitting the cheese
- ✓ Swapping the cheese for a cashew nut cheese either shop bought or homemade (or any other vegan cheese you have to hand)
- ✓ Replacing the butter with olive oil

I also use coconut sugar and tamari sauce in my recipes because I personally do not consume gluten or cane sugar, but please feel free to use soy sauce and cane sugar if it's easier for you.

When tackling a recipe for the first time, it is a good idea to work carefully though the ingredients list, prepare all the ingredients and then follow the method for constructing your salad. This will keep everything organized and make sure you don't miss anything.

Finally, if you prefer one vegetable to another or really don't like something, then add in more of one and less of the other, or omit it completely and/or swap it for something else. Lunch in a Jar is designed to give you more freedom, not less!

This cookbook is meant to be an easy and flexible approach to cooking to suit your needs.

Quick kitchen conversion

Please find below a quick reference guide to key measurements and oven temperatures.

Tsp. = teaspoon = 5ml
Tbsp. = tablespoon = 15ml
3 tsp. = 1 tbsp.
250ml = 1 cup

Oven temperature conversions

Celcius	Fan Oven	Fahrenheit	Gas Mark
140°C	120°C	275°F	1
150°C	130°C	300°F	2
170°C	150°C	325°F	3
180°C	160°C	350°F	4
190°C	170°C	375°F	5
200°C	180°C	400°F	6
220°C	200°C	425°F	7
230°C	210°C	450°F	8
240°C	220°C	475°F	9
260°C	240°C	500°F	10

About the author

Fiona Manning is a qualified nutritionist who is fascinated by the link between lifestyle and health. Having successfully overcome chronic fatigue and adrenal exhaustion, she now wants to help others make the breakthrough to a more energetic life by understanding the importance diet plays in optimum health. After years of research she has concluded that by taking just a little better care of ourselves inside and out, we can combat many health issues naturally through the food we eat. Simply by making a few changes – such as including a little more fruit and vegetables into our daily diet – we can start the ball rolling towards becoming a healthier and happier version of ourselves.

CHAPTER 1
Sub-Recipes

How to use this section

Using the following techniques for cooking vegetables turns plain vegetables into exciting additions to any meal. These sub-recipes explain to you simple methods of preparing a variety of vegetables, nuts, seeds and spices. If a recipe requires you to use one of the following methods then it will direct you back to this section. The recipes below can also be used independently as accompaniments to other dishes.

1. BLANCHED VEGETABLES: MANGE TOUT, GREEN BEANS, BROCOLI, CURLY KALE AND PEAS

Blanching is a quick and easy way to cook vegetables while preserving that peak crunch and taste. It also makes the color much more vibrant. I think vegetables prepared in this way for salads taste much nicer than their raw counterparts and they give bulk without calories. 100g of green beans will add 32 calories to your lunch pot whereas 100g of feta will add 262 calories. This doesn't mean skip the feta - just balance it out with extra veg if you want to reduce the calories of your meals! For the green beans I would top and tail them and chop them into 3, making them more manageable to eat when you are on the move. The same with the broccoli: chop it into manageable bite-size pieces before boiling.

Method:

1. Bring a saucepan of water to boil with a little salt.
2. Once water is boiling add your vegetables depending on what recipe you are following.
3. Leave in for one to two minutes depending on preference. The longer you leave them in the less crunchy they will be.
4. Drain and run under a cold tap or stick the vegetables into a bowl of ice water to stop them cooking any further.

2. ROASTED NUTS: HAZELNUTS, WALNUTS, ALMONDS, CASHEW NUTS AND PINENUTS

I love roasting nuts, I think it changes their flavour completely for the better, making them nuttier and crunchier! They are great added to salads for a boost of flavour and some extra bite. I roast them dry as I don't feel you need to add any oil to improve flavour or texture. You can also choose to roast a small batch that will keep for a couple of days in an airtight container in the fridge. If you enjoy snacking on nuts or know that you will use them in other dishes it saves you time having a batch ready to use.

Method:

1. Preheat oven to 175°C (see table on page 12 for oven conversions)

2. Line a baking tray with parchment paper.
3. Spread nuts on tray.
4. Roast for 5-10 minutes, turning occasionally (pine nuts will only need 5 minutes).
5. Allow to cool completely before using.

3. SPICED ROASTED PUMPKIN

I think this is a brilliant way of cooking pumpkin, the roasting enhances the flavour and adding maple syrup gives it a lovely caramelised finish. It is also a great healthy snack by itself so feel free to double the recipe and save the rest for when you are feeling a little bit peckish.

You will need 1/4 of a pumpkin peeled and cubed, 1 tbsp. of cumin seeds, 1 tbsp. of maple syrup, 2 tbsp. of olive oil, pinch of cayenne powder, salt and pepper to taste

Method:

1. Preheat oven to 220°C (see table on page 12 for oven conversions)
2. In an oiled baking tray combine the cubed pumpkin with the olive oil, cumin seeds, cayenne pepper, maple syrup and salt and pepper.
3. Bake for 35-40 minutes turning occasionally (the pumpkin is cooked when it looks caramelised).
4. Set aside to cool.

4. GRILLED PEPPERS AND COURGETTES

Grilling peppers gives them a much sweeter taste. I think they add an exciting edge to salads and mix really well with feta or goat's cheese. My mum grills them and then marinates them in balsamic vinegar and olive oil and serves them at BBQ's. I only use courgettes and peppers grilled in the following recipes but it works just as well for aubergine. I usually use a whole courgette and a whole pepper and anything I don't use in my salad, I save for later either as an afternoon snack or to accompany my dinner.

Method:

1. Preheat grill.
2. Cut courgette into 3 and slice thinly long-ways.
3. Cut the pepper into quarters and de-seed.
4. Line a baking tin with foil.
5. Depending on whether you are preparing both or just one of these ingredients, spread them out onto the tray making sure none of them are overlapping.
6. Drizzle with olive oil and sprinkle with salt and pepper.
7. Grill 10-15 minutes on each side or until the courgette look crisp but not burned, and pepper skins have started to charcoal (the more charcoaled they are the easier it is to take the skin off).

8. Remove from heat, and wrap the peppers tightly in cling film.
9. Set aside and allow to cool for a couple of minutes before removing the skins from the peppers. At this point I usually slice them into thinner strips

5. ROASTED OR TOASTED PUMPKIN SEEDS

Traditionally pumpkin seeds are roasted. I find it quicker and easier to dry fry them, although you will want to keep an eye on them as they can quickly burn. You will know when they are ready because they will have popped and swollen up. I find pumpkin seeds have got so much more flavour when toasted, it gives them a lovely nutty taste and I love the crunchiness they add to salads. They also make for a great tasting, low calorie snack, I usually eat them plain but you can add anything from the following list to spice them up and make them more exciting: sea salt, pepper, garlic salt, cumin, paprika, celery salt, ground cinnamon, ginger, cloves or a drizzle of olive oil.

Pan-frying method:

1. Heat frying pan.
2. Add a handful of pumpkin seeds, or however many you want to use (you can make a large batch and store them in an airtight container for a couple of days).
3. Dry fry for 3-4 minutes until they have popped and swollen up.
4. Remove from heat and leave to cool.

Roasted method:

Follow recipe for roasted nuts on page 14.

6. ROASTED BEETROOT

I cannot emphasize enough how different cooking methods change the taste, flavour and texture of your vegetables! Beetroot is one of those vegetables for which roasting really changes everything about it. I find the flavour is enhanced and I love the chewy cooked texture. It is also great combined with goat's cheese and a little honey. You can even drizzle a little honey on the beetroot before roasting for additional sweetness and chewiness! I would usually use one beetroot per person/meal.

Method:

1. Preheat oven to 220°C (see table on page 12 for oven conversions).
2. Peel beetroot and cut into six segments.
3. Place on an oiled baking tray.
4. Drizzle with olive oil.
5. Sprinkle with salt and pepper.
6. Bake for approximately 25 minutes or until crispy and tender.
7. Set aside to cool.

7. DRY FRYING AND GRINDING CUMIN, CORIANDER, MUSTARD AND SESAME SEEDS

There are two main reasons to dry fry cumin and coriander seeds. The first is that it drives off excess moisture making the seeds crispier and easier to grind. The second is that it helps maximize flavour by releasing the oils giving a more intense, earthy flavour.

Method

1. Heat a medium-sized frying pan.
2. Add seeds to pan.
3. Fry over a medium heat, stirring constantly (2-3 minutes).
4. Seeds are ready when they start to brown and a warm aroma is released.
5. Remove from heat.
6. Seeds are ready to use, crush in either a pestle and mortar or coffee grinder if recipe requires ground spices.

CHAPTER 2
Vegetarian and Vegan Lunch Pots

BLUE CHEESE, PEAR AND HAZELNUT SALAD POT

This is a lovely light salad pot. The pear combined with the blue cheese and the roasted hazelnuts give it a beautiful distinct flavour, with the radishes and mange tout adding that little bit of crunch.

Prep Time: 20 minutes | Servings: 1 | Difficulty: Easy

Gf Ef V Sf Gf

Ingredients:

For the dressing
2 tbsp. of cold pressed olive oil
1 tbsp. of balsamic vinegar
Salt and pepper to taste

For the Salad
55g of mange tout, blanched (see page 14)
60g (4) radishes, sliced thinly
45g (1/4) red pepper, diced
40g (1/4) avocado, diced
40g (1/4) a pear, diced
50g blue cheese, crumbled
20g of hazelnuts, roasted (see page 14)
50g rocket

Method:

1. Add salad dressing ingredients to bottom of jar and mix well.
2. Add in the mange tout, radishes, red pepper, avocado and pear.
3. Top with the blue cheese, hazelnuts and the rocket.
4. Refrigerate until needed.
5. When ready to eat turn upside down to mix in salad dressing.

SPICED ROASTED PUMPKIN AND GOAT'S CHEESE SALAD POT

This is a brilliant autumn salad, pumpkin is naturally sweet and full of vitamin A and C, cooking the pumpkin with maple syrup and cayenne pepper gives in a sweet spicy medley of flavours, combining beautifully with the goat's cheese and grilled vegetables!

Prep Time: 20 minutes | Cook time: 40 minutes| Servings: 1 | Difficulty: Medium

Gf Ef V Sf Gf

Ingredients:

Spiced pumpkin
260g pumpkin, peeled and diced
2 tsp. of cumin seeds, dry fried (see page 17)
2 tsp. of maple syrup
1 tbsp. of olive oil
Pinch of ground cayenne pepper
Salt and pepper to taste

Salad dressing
2 tbsp. of cold pressed olive oil
1 tbsp. of balsamic vinegar
Salt and pepper to taste

Salad
110g (1/4) courgette, grilled (see page 15)
80g (1/2) pepper mixed red and yellow, grilled (see page 15)
50g goat's cheese, cubed
20g roasted walnuts (see page 14)
10g toasted pumpkin seeds (see page 16)
15g rocket

Method:

1. Preheat oven to 180°C (see table on page 12 for oven conversions)
2. In a medium-sized baking tray mix the pumpkin, cumin seeds, maple syrup, olive oil, cayenne pepper and salt and pepper until well combined.
3. Bake for 35-40 minutes, turning occasionally, until the squash is golden brown.
4. Add salad dressing ingredients to bottom of jar and mix well to combine.
5. Put the grilled courgette and peppers into the jar, followed by the goats; cheese, walnuts, pumpkin seeds and rocket.
6. Once the pumpkin has cooled, add to jar.
7. Refrigerate until needed.
8. When ready to eat turn upside down to mix in salad dressing.

ROASTED BEETROOT, GOAT'S CHEESE AND WALNUT SALAD POT

This is a really nice way to eat beetroot. Roasting the beetroot caramelises it, giving it a sweet yet earthy flavour. Adding goat's cheese and walnuts complements these flavours, making this a tasty winter salad and one of my favourites!

Prep Time: 15 minutes | Cook Time: 25 minutes | Servings: 1 Serving | Difficulty: Easy

Gf Ef V Sf Gf

Ingredients:

For the salad
70g (1) medium beetroot, cut into eighths, roasted (see page 16)
50g (3) radishes, sliced thinly
60g of green beans, blanched and cut into thirds (see page 14)
40g (1/4) red pepper, sliced
80g (1/2) avocado, diced
50g goat's cheese, cubed
20g walnuts, roasted (see page 14)
30g rocket

For the dressing
2 tbsp. of cold pressed olive oil
1 tbsp. of balsamic vinegar
1 tsp. of honey
Salt and pepper to taste

Method:

1. Pre heat oven to 220°C (see table on page 12 for oven conversions) and follow recipe on page 16 for roasting beetroot.
2. Add the salad dressing ingredients to bottom of jar and mix well to combine.
3. Put the radishes, green beans, red pepper and avocado into the jar.
4. Top with the goats' cheese, walnuts and rocket,
5. Once the beetroot has cooled, add to jar.
6. Refrigerate until needed.
7. When ready to eat turn upside down to mix in salad dressing.

POTATO, GARDEN PEA AND CHIVE SALAD POT WITH LEMON BUTTER DRESSING

The idea for this recipe came from the Body Ecology lemon butter sauce, I had it once with potatoes whilst on the diet and loved it! It's just a bit different from all the standard salad dressings and the lemon and tarragon really bring out the other flavours in the salad.

Prep Time: 20 minutes | Cook Time: 20 minutes | Servings: 1 | Difficulty: Medium

Gf Ef V Sf Gf Nf

Ingredients:

For the salad
80g (2) red potatoes, diced into small cubes
80g garden peas (frozen), blanched (see page 16)
40g (4) cherry tomatoes, halved
49g (1/4) avocado, cubed
3 Sun dried-tomatoes, sliced thinly
47g (1/4) red pepper, diced
20g pumpkin seeds, toasted (see page 16)
1 tbsp. fresh tarragon, finely chopped
1 tbsp. of fresh chives (or 1 tsp. of dried)
2 tsp. of apple cider vinegar
1/2 lemon (juice)

For the dressing
50g butter
2 tsp. of cold pressed olive oil
1/2 an onion, thinly chopped
1/4 tsp. of dried tarragon or 1/2 tbsp. finely torn fresh tarragon
1 lemon, juice
Salt and pepper to taste

Method:

1. Put the cubed potatoes into a pan of cold water, bring to the boil, and simmer for approximately 20 minutes until potatoes are cooked and set aside.
2. In a medium-sized frying pan melt the butter and olive oil, add the onions and sauté until soft. Add the lemon juice, tarragon and salt and pepper. Simmer for approximately 6-8 minutes, until sauce has reduced and thickened.
3. In a medium-sized bowl put the garden peas, cherry tomatoes, avocado, red pepper, fresh tarragon, chives, apple cider vinegar and lemon juice.
4. Once ready add the potatoes and lemon butter dressing to the bowl, mix well, and add all to jar.
5. Refrigerate until needed.

Notes: I use red skin potatoes in this recipe because they are lower in sugar but any kind of potato will work. I also keep the skins on for extra nutrition, as potato skins provide fibre, flavonoids and other nutrients.

ROASTED ROOT VEGETABLE FETA AND TOASTED PINE NUT SALAD POT

I love the rustic feel of this salad, roasted vegetables to me taste just as good cold as they do hot! A great salad for winter as it is more substantial for those cold winter months than a lighter leafy green one. You can even double up on the quantities and enjoy one straight from the oven as an accompaniment to your evening meal.

Prep Time: 10 minutes | Cook Time: 40 minutes | Servings: 1 | Difficulty: Easy

Gf Ef V Sf Gf

Ingredients:

Roasted vegetables
160g (1) sweet potatoes, peeled and diced
100g (1/2) medium courgette, cubed
50g (1/2) a red pepper, diced
75g (1) medium carrot, peeled and diced
75g (1) parsnip, peeled and diced
80g (1) beetroot, peeled and diced
1 tbsp. olive oil
Salt and pepper to taste

For the salad
20g pine nuts, toasted (see page 14)
60g of feta, cubed

Method:

1. Preheat oven to 180°C (see table on page 12 for oven conversions)
2. In a medium-sized baking tray put the sweet potato, courgette, red pepper, carrot, parsnip and beetroot, drizzle with olive oil, salt & pepper, and toss well.
3. Bake, stirring occasionally, for approximately 35-40 minutes until cooked. Allow to cool.
4. In a medium-sized mixing bowl combine roasted vegetables, feta and pine nuts/ Transfer to jar.
5. Refrigerate pot until needed.

ASIAN SLAW AND GINGER PEANUT DRESSING SALAD POT

If you love peanut butter, you will love this recipe. It's like an awesome vegetable platter but in a jar. The raw vegetables mixed with the peanut and ginger dressing gives it a perfect sweet-nutty-salty-sour mix of flavours.

Prep Time: 15 minutes | Servings: 1 serving | Difficulty: Easy

Gf Ef V Sf Gf Df

Ingredients:

For the dressing
1 tbsp. of cold pressed olive oil
1 tbsp. sesame oil
1 tbsp. peanut butter
1 tbsp. tamari sauce
1 tsp. honey
4g (1/8) red chilli, diced thinly
1 clove of garlic, crushed
4g fresh ginger (small piece), peeled and minced
Fresh coriander (1 Sprig) finely chopped

For the salad
30g (handful) curly kale, thick stems removed and blanched (see page 14)
70g red cabbage, shredded
25g (1/5) red pepper, sliced thinly
50g (1/2) carrot, peeled and sliced thinly
25g cashew nuts, roasted (see page 14)

Method:

1. Add dressing ingredients to bottom of jar and mix well to combine.
2. Add cabbage, blanched kale, red pepper and carrot.
3. Top with toasted cashew nuts.
4. Refrigerate until needed.
5. When ready to eat turn upside down to mix in salad dressing.

THAI MANGO AND ROASTED CASHEW NUT SALAD POT

This is a beautiful, light summer salad pot bursting with oriental flavours. The sweet mango enhances the fresh mint and the hot chilli, making it a low calorie but highly flavoursome dish.

Prep Time: 15 minutes | Cook Time: 5-10 minutes | Servings: 1 | Difficulty: Easy

Gf Ef V Sf Gf Df

Ingredients:

For the dressing
1 tbsp. olive oil
1 tbsp. sesame oil
1/2 lime rind zest and juice
1 tbsp. tamari sauce
1 tsp. honey
1 clove of garlic
4g (1/8) red chilli pepper
4g (small piece) fresh ginger, peeled and minced
Salt and pepper to taste

For the salad
80g (1/2) a mango, diced
30g (1/4) red pepper, sliced thinly
30g (1/2) carrot, sliced thinly
30g (1/3) courgette, thinly sliced
49g (1/4) avocado, diced
Fresh mint (2 sprigs), finely chopped
Fresh coriander (2 sprigs), finely chopped
Fresh basil (2 sprigs), finely chopped
25g cashew nuts, roasted (see page 14)

Method:

1. Combine all dressing ingredients in bottom of jar and mix well.
2. In a medium-sized mixing bowl, combine all salad ingredients except the cashew nuts, mix well and transfer to jar.
3. Top with roasted cashew nuts.
3. Refrigerate until needed.
4. When ready to eat turn upside down to mix in salad dressing.

ROASTED PEPPER FETA AND PINE NUT SALAD POT

This salad pot is Greek inspired. With its Mediterranean feel, it is a great light lunch for those hot summer months, but can also be enjoyed all year round. The tanginess of the feta cheese with the sweetness of the roasted peppers make for an amazing combination.

Prep Time: 20 minutes | Cook Time: 10-15 minutes | Servings: 1 | Difficulty: Medium

Gf Ef V Sf Gf

Ingredients:

For the salad
120g (1/2) red pepper, grilled (see page 15)
120g (1/2) yellow pepper, grilled (see page 15)
60g Feta, diced
35g pitted olives (green and/or black)
25g (1/4) red onion, sliced thinly
49g (1/4) avocado, diced
20g Pine nuts, roasted
30g Rocket
Fresh basil (1 sprig), finely chopped

For the dressing
2 tbsp. of cold pressed olive oil
1 tbsp. balsamic vinegar
1/2 tsp. honey
Salt and pepper to taste

Method:

1. Prepare peppers following recipe on page 15.
2. Combine all dressing ingredients in bottom of jar and mix well.
3. In a medium-sized mixing bowl combine the peppers, feta, olives, onion, avocado, pine nuts and basil, mix well, and transfer to jar.
4. Top with rocket.
5. Refrigerate salad pot until needed.
6. When ready to eat turn upside down to mix in salad dressing.

SPICY MEXICAN BEAN SALAD POT

This tasty mixed bean salad has a really nice kick to it. Colourful, vibrant, and refreshing, this lunch pot contains just the right amount of sweet and spice.

Prep Time: 15 minutes | Servings: 1 | Difficulty: Easy

Gf Ef V Sf Gf Vg Nf Df

Ingredients:

For the dressing
2 tbsp. of cold pressed olive oil 1 tsp. red wine vinegar
1/2 lime, rind and juice
1/2 lemon, rind and juice
2 tsp. coconut sugar
1 garlic clove, crushed
1/8 tsp. cayenne pepper
Salt and pepper to taste

For the salad
50g of cooked kidney beans
50g of cooked cannellini beans
50g (1/2) a red pepper, diced
50g (1/2) green pepper, diced
60g of sweet corn
25g (1/4) a red onion, chopped thinly
49g (1/4) avocado, diced
6 cherry tomatoes, cut into quarters
4g (1/8) of red chilli, chopped thinly
Fresh coriander (2 sprigs), finely chopped

Method:

1. In a large mixing bowl combine all the salad dressing ingredients and mix well.
2. Add the red kidney beans, cannellini beans, red and green pepper, sweet corn, red onion, avocado, tomatoes, chilli and coriander, mix well and transfer to jar.
3. Refrigerate salad pot until needed.
4. When ready to eat turn upside down to mix in salad dressing.

GRAPE, AVOCADO AND GOAT'S CHEESE SALAD POT

This is a light, refreshing salad. The sweetness of the grapes provides a wonderful contrast to the distinct, tart, earthy flavour of the goat's cheese. The crunchiness of the roasted walnuts finish off this dish perfectly, complementing both the grapes and the goats' cheese.

Prep Time: 15 minutes | Cook Time: 5-10 minutes | Servings: 1 | Difficulty: Easy

Gf Ef V Sf Gf

Ingredients:

For the dressing
2 tbsp. of cold pressed olive oil
1 tbsp. balsamic vinegar
1 tsp. honey
Salt and pepper to taste

For the salad
120g grapes, halved
160g (1/2) avocado, diced
27g (1/4) red onion, finely diced
60g goat's cheese, sliced
30g walnuts, roasted (see page 14)
30g rocket

Method:

1. Combine all dressing ingredients in bottom of jar and mix well.
2. Add the grapes, avocado and red onion to the jar.
3. Top with goat's cheese, roasted walnuts and rocket.
4. Refrigerate until needed.
5. When ready to eat turn upside down to mix in salad dressing.

GREEK SALAD POT

The classic Greek salad, this pot is simple yet glorious. The fruity olive mix and tangy feta make for a perfect combination and one that has stood the test of time.

Prep Time: 15 minutes | Servings: 1 | Difficulty: Easy

Gf Ef V Sf Gf Nf

Ingredients:

For the dressing
2 tbsp. of cold pressed olive oil
1 tbsp. red wine vinegar
1 tsp. Dijon mustard
1 glove of garlic, crushed
1/4 tsp. dried oregano
1 tsp. capers
Fresh basil (2 sprig), finely chopped
1/2 lemon, juice
Salt and pepper to taste

For the salad
25g (1/4) red pepper, diced
25g (1/4) yellow pepper, diced
60g (6) cherry tomatoes quartered
30g (1/4) cucumber de-seeded and diced
160g (1/2) avocado, diced
27g (1/4) red onion, diced
50g pitted olives (black and green)
65g Feta, diced

Method:

1. Combine all dressing ingredients in bottom of jar and mix well.
2. In a large mixing bowl combine the red pepper, yellow pepper, cherry tomatoes, cucumber, avocado, red onion, olives and feta, and mix well.
3. Transfer to jar.
4. Refrigerate salad pot until needed.
5. When ready to eat turn upside down to mix in salad dressing.

CURRIED ROASTED VEGETABLE, CHICKPEA, MINT AND FETA SALAD POT

The combination of chickpeas and root vegetables roasted in honey and spices, and topped with feta and cashew nuts makes for a tasty Moroccan-style lunch that is simply bursting with flavour.

Prep Time: 15 minutes | Cook Time: 40 minutes | Servings: 1 | Difficulty: Medium

Gf Ef V Sf Gf

Ingredients:

For the marinade
2 tbsp. of cold pressed olive oil
2 tsp. cumin seeds, dry fried and crushed (see page 17)
1 tsp. coriander seeds, dry fried and crushed (see page 17)
1/4 tsp. ground ginger
1/4 tsp. ground cinnamon
1/8 tsp. cayenne pepper
1 tsp. honey

For the salad
195g (1) sweet potatoes, peeled
112g (1) courgette
40g 1/2 red pepper
40g 1/2 green pepper
75g (1) carrot
135g (1) parsnip
120g (1/2) tin of chickpeas
40g of feta, cubed
Fresh mint (2 sprig), finely chopped
1 tsp. (drizzle) olive oil
30g cashew nuts, roasted (see page 14)

Method:

1. Preheat oven to 220°C (see table on page 12 for oven conversions)
2. Chop the sweet potato, courgette, red and green pepper, carrot and parsnip into small chunks.
3. In a large bowl mix together all the marinade ingredients.
3. Add the sweet potato, courgette, red and green pepper, carrot and parsnip and mix well.
4. Transfer to oiled baking tray, bake for approximately 40 minutes until potatoes are soft and crisp, turning every 10-15 minutes. Add chickpeas to roasted vegetables after the first 20 minutes.
5. Once cooked, set aside to cool.
6. Transfer to jar, top with feta, mint and cashew nuts, and drizzle with olive oil.
7. Refrigerate salad pot until needed.

RED LENTIL AND COCONUT CURRY POT

A nourishing, hearty and warming curry packed full of delicious Indian flavours. Low in calories and high in nutrition, feel free to top with a little steamed broccoli for some added nourishment. A must try this winter!

Prep Time: 15 minutes | Cook Time: 30 minutes | Servings: 1 | Difficulty: Medium

Gf Ef V VG Sf Gf Df

Ingredients:

For spice mix
2 tsp. coriander seeds, dry fried and crushed (see page 17)
1 tbsp. cumin seeds, dry fried and crushed (see page 17)
1 tsp. ground turmeric
1/4 tsp. ground clove
1/4 tsp. ground cinnamon
1/4 tsp. ground cayenne pepper
2 garlic cloves, crushed
1/2 fresh chili, chopped thinly
2 tbsp. of olive oil

For the curry
70g (1) onion, finely chopped
200g (1 cup) red split lentils (check to see if they need to be pre-soaked), rinsed
95g (1/3) courgette, diced
84g (1) carrot, peeled and diced
400ml water (3 cups)
1 tbsp. tomato paste
150g coconut milk
1 lime (juice)
2 tbsp. tamari sauce
20g cashew nuts, roasted (see page 14) *optional*
70g (2 florets) broccoli, blanched (see page 14) *optional*

Method:

1. In a medium-sized mixing bowl, combine all the ingredients for the spice mix well to combine.
2. Heat a large saucepan, add the olive oil, onion and spice mix, and fry for 3-5 minutes until onion is translucent, stirring frequently.
3. Add the carrot and courgette and fry for a further 5 minutes.
4. Add the lentils, water and tomato paste.
5. Bring to the boil, reduce heat, and simmer for 15 minutes or until lentils are tender.
6. Add the coconut milk, tamari sauce and lime juice, and simmer for a further 5 minutes before removing from heat
7. Once cool, transfer to jar. If using cashew nuts keep separate until curry has been reheated and is ready to be eaten.
8. Top with broccoli *optional*.
9. Refrigerate until needed.
10. Reheat before serving; top with cashew nuts *optional*.

Notes: This recipe does not use salt, if you choose to use it only add it in at the end, salt added in at the beginning of cooking will toughen the lentils.

SWEET POTATO AND CHICKPEA CURRY POT

The sweet potato and coconut milk add a sweet creaminess to this dish balancing out the flavours from the spice mix. Add in the chickpeas and we have a perfect fusion of Indian and West African cuisine. A wonderful, heart-warming curry!

Prep Time: 15 minutes | Cook Time: 40 minutes | Servings: 1 | Difficulty: Medium

Gf Ef V VG Sf Gf Df

Ingredients:

For spice mix
2 tsp. coriander seeds, dry fried and crushed (see page 17)
2 tsp. cumin seeds, dry fried and crushed (see page 17)
1/2 tsp. ground turmeric
1/2 tsp. ground clove
1/2 tsp. ground ginger
1/2 tsp. ground cinnamon
2 garlic cloves, crushed
4g (1/8) fresh chili, deseeded chopped thinly
2 tbsp. olive oil

For the curry
54g (1/2) onion, finely chopped
50g (1/2) red pepper, diced
195g (1) sweet potato, peeled and diced
300ml water
120g (1) tomato, chopped
120g chickpeas
100ml coconut milk
1/2 lime, juice
1 tbsp. tamari sauce
Salt and pepper
70g broccoli (2 florets), blanched (see page 14) *optional*

Method:

1. In a medium-sized mixing bowl, combine all the ingredients for the spice mix well to combine.
2. Heat a large saucepan, add the olive oil, onion and spice mix. Fry for 3-5 minutes until onion is translucent, stirring frequently.
3. Add the diced sweet potato and red pepper. Fry for a further 3 minutes.
4. Add the water and chopped tomato.
5. Bring to the boil, reduce heat and cook for approximately 25-30 minutes until the sweet potato is soft.
6. Add the coconut milk, tamari sauce and lime juice, and simmer for a further 5 minutes before removing from the heat.
7. Once cool transfer to jar.
8. Top with broccoli *optional*.
9. Refrigerate until needed.
10. Reheat before serving.

CHAPTER 3
Fish Lunch Pots

ORANGE AND THYME POACHED SALMON AND ENDIVE SALAD POT

Poaching in a fruity liquid is a wonderful way to cook salmon. The sweetness of the orange infuses the fish and complements the endives. A little sweet, a bit of tang, a hint of bitter and a touch of citrus, this dish is perfect for brightening up a bleak winter day.

Prep Time: 30 minutes | Cook Time: 25 minutes | Servings: 1 | Difficulty: Medium

Gf Ef Sf Gf Df

Ingredients:

For the poached salmon
1 orange, zest whole and use half for segments and the other half for juice
177 ml (3/4 cup) of water
1 piece of fresh salmon
125g (1) endive
1/2 tsp. of black peppercorns
2 sprigs of fresh thyme
Salt and pepper

For the salad
60g (3 heads) broccoli, cut small and blanched (see page 14) 50g (1/2) of a red pepper, grilled (see page 15)
80g (1/4) of an avocado, cubed
40g cherry tomatoes, halved
25g pine nuts or almonds, roasted (see page 14)

Method:

1. Put orange juice, water, orange zest, thyme, peppercorns and salt and pepper in a large saucepan, bring to the boil, reduce heat and simmer for 5 minutes.
2. Add the whole endive, cover and cook for approximately 10 minutes or until tender, remove from heat, set aside to cool and slice into chunks.
3. In the same liquid add the salmon, cover and cook for approximately 10-12 minutes until firm and flaky.
4. Once salmon is cooked remove from liquid and set aside to cool before slicing into chunks.
5. Keep liquid over heat and reduce to a thicker consistency.
6. Add the sauce produced to jar, followed by salmon pieces, orange segments and endives.
7. Top with broccoli, red pepper, avocado, cherry tomatoes and pine nuts or almonds.
8. Refrigerate salad pot until needed.
9. When ready to eat turn upside down to mix in sauce (can be eaten hot or cold).

SEARED TUNA STEAK, SUN-DRIED TOMATO, SWEET CORN AND WALNUT SALAD POT

This Mediterranean-inspired dish is bursting with flavour. The pleasant tartness of the capers and the intense, slightly salty flavour of the sun-dried tomatoes help complement the richness of the fish. A delightful and satisfying lunchtime option!

Prep Time: 20 minutes | Cook Time: 7 minutes | Servings: 1 | Difficulty: Medium

Gf Ef Sf Gf Df

Ingredients:

For the dressing
2 tbsp. olive oil
1 tbsp. red wine vinegar
1/2 tsp. wholegrain mustard
1 clove garlic, crushed
1/2 lemon, juice
Salt pepper

For the tuna
1 tsp. olive oil
1 piece of fresh tuna (can be substituted for a small tin of tuna flakes)
1/2 tsp. cracked black pepper
Salt

For the salad
65g green beans, blanched (see page 14), sliced into 3
35g (1/3) red pepper, diced
65g (1/5) cucumber, diced
50g (2 tbsp.) sweet corn
30g sun-dried tomatoes (3), sliced
25g (1) spring onion, sliced
5g capers
10g pumpkin seeds, roasted
20g walnuts, roasted
20g rocket

Method:

1. Combine all salad dressing ingredients in bottom of jar and mix well.
2. In a medium-sized mixing bowl, add the green beans, red pepper, cucumber, sweet corn, sun dried tomatoes, spring onion and capers, stir together and set aside.
3. Press the cracked black pepper on both sides of the tuna steak and sprinkle lightly with salt *
4. Heat olive oil in a medium frying pan over a medium-to-high heat.
5. Add tuna and cook according to preference (3 1/2 minutes on each side for medium).
6. Once cooled, slice tuna thinly and add to jar.
7. Top with salad ingredients from mixing bowl.
8. Add the pumpkin seeds, walnuts and rocket.
9. Refrigerate until needed.
10. When ready to eat turn upside down to mix in salad dressing.

If using tinned tuna, add straight to mixing bowl with other salad ingredients and skip steps 3-6

THAI SPICED SALMON SALAD POT

This Thai-inspired salad has a beautiful aromatic fragrance thanks to the lemongrass, chilli, garlic and lime. In combination with the rest of the salad dressing ingredients it creates the perfect balance of sour, sweet, bitter and salty. Fresh, healthy and full of flavour, this makes for a great summer time lunch!

Prep Time: 20 minutes | Cook Time: 15 minutes | Servings: 1 | Difficulty: Medium

Gf Ef Sf Gf Df

Ingredients:

Salad dressing
1 tbsp. sesame oil
2g of lemon grass
1/2 tsp. of fish sauce
3 tsp. of tamari sauce
1 tsp. of apple cider vinegar
1 tsp. of maple of syrup
4g (1/8) of fresh red chilli, finely chopped
1 clove of garlic, crushed
1 sprig of basil (6 leaves), finely chopped
4g of fresh ginger (small piece), peeled and minced
Fresh coriander (1 sprig), finely chopped
1/2 a lime, juice

For the salad
1 piece of salmon
40g (1/4) avocado, diced
50g (3) radish, quartered
40g mange tout, blanched (see page 14)
65g carrot, cut into strips
30g red pepper, cut into strips
25g cashew nuts, roasted (see page 14)

Method:

1. Preheat oven at 180°C (see table on page 12 for oven conversions)
2. Place salmon on an oiled baking tray, drizzle with olive oil, season with salt and pepper and bake for approximately 15 minutes or until cooked. Set aside to cool.
3. Add all dressing ingredients to bottom of jar and mix well.
4. Slice salmon and add to jar.
5. Follow with avocado, radishes, mange tout, carrots and red pepper.
6. Top with roasted cashew nuts.
7. Refrigerate until needed.
8. When ready to eat turn upside down to mix in salad dressing.

TUNA, TARRAGON AND BUTTERBEAN SALAD POT

Whip up this salad in minutes, perfect for those lazy evenings. Easy yet full of flavour, this salad is even better the following day. The distinct sweet anise-like flavour of the tarragon makes this salad unique. High in protein and low GI this hearty lunch will satisfy those hungry taste buds!

Prep Time: 15 minutes | Difficulty: Easy

Gf Ef Sf Gf Df Nf

Ingredients:

For the salad
1 small tin of tuna flakes (60g)
120g (1/2) can of butter beans, rinsed
1 tsp. capers
80g green beans, blanched (see page 14), cut into thirds
27g (1/4) red onion, sliced
50g (1/2) red pepper, sliced
40g (4) cherry tomatoes, quartered
60g (4) radishes, sliced
2 sprigs fresh tarragon leaves, chopped finely
1 clove of garlic, crushed
1/2 lemon, zest and juice
2 tbsp. olive oil
1 tbsp. apple cider vinegar
Salt and pepper

Method:

1. In a bowl, mix together the butter beans, tuna, capers, green beans, red onion, red pepper, cherry tomatoes and radishes.
2. Add olive oil, garlic, tarragon, apple cider vinegar, lemon zest and juice and salt and pepper to taste. Mix well.
3. Transfer to jar.
4. Refrigerate until needed.

CURRY SPICED SALMON, CELERY AND GRAPE SALAD POT

This is a delicious spicy coconut salmon lunch packed full of flavour! The celery gives it a fantastic crunch and the sweet grapes complement the heat of the chilli.

Prep Time: 25 minutes | Cook Time: 15 minutes | Servings: 1 Serving | Difficulty: Easy

Gf Ef Sf Gf Df

Ingredients:

For the salad
1 piece of salmon
120g red grapes, halved
86g (1 stick) of celery sticks, sliced
40g (1/4) avocado, cubed
20g almonds sliced and roasted (see page 14)

For the dressing
1 tsp. cumin seeds, dry fried and crushed (see page 17)
1 tsp. coriander seeds, dry fried and crushed (see page 17)
1/4 tsp. ground cinnamon
1/2 tsp. ground turmeric
1 tbsp. of sesame oil
2 tsp. tamari sauce
1 tsp. of honey
1 clove of garlic, crushed
4g (1/8) red chili, chopped thinly
3 tbsp. Coconut milk

Method:

1. Preheat oven at 180°C (see table on page 12 for oven conversions)
2. Place salmon on an oiled baking tray, drizzle with olive oil, season with salt and pepper and bake for approximately 15 minutes or until cooked.
3. In a large mixing bowl, combine all the dressing ingredients and mix well.
4. Once the salmon is cooked, allow to cool, slice and add to bowl along with the rest of the salad ingredients, mix well and transfer to jar.
5. Top with almonds.
6. Refrigerate until needed.

CHAPTER 4
Chicken Lunch Pots

SPICY CHICKEN, MANGO AND GRAPE SALAD POT

Fresh, healthy and exotic, this lightly spiced chicken fruit salad has a nice balance of savory and sweet. Simple and easy to make, there is something about mango and chicken together that just works.

Prep Time: 30 minutes | Cook Time: 20 minutes | Servings: 1 | Difficulty: Medium

Gf Ef Sf Gf Df

Ingredients:

For the salad
1 skinless chicken breast
2 tsp. olive oil
80g red grapes, sliced
75g mango, diced
30g (1/4) red pepper, diced
65g (1/5) cucumber, diced
40g (1/4) avocado, diced
40g (1/4) red onion, diced
20g cashew nuts roasted, (see page 14)

For the dressing
4 tsp. toasted sesame seed oil
4 tsp. tamari sauce
1 lime (juice)
2 tsp. honey
2 clove garlic, crushed
1/8 red chilli, seeded and finely chopped
8g ginger grated
Fresh coriander (1 sprig), finely chopped

Method:

1. Rub 1 tsp. olive oil into the chicken breast and season with salt and pepper.
2. Heat the rest of the olive oil in a medium frying pan, add the chicken and cook for approximately 10 minutes on each side until golden brown on the outside and cooked in the middle. Set aside to cool.
3. Combine all dressing ingredients in the bottom of the jar and mix well.
4. Slice the chicken and add to the bottom of the jar, followed by the red grapes, red pepper, avocado, red onion and cashew nuts.
5. Refrigerate until needed.
6. When ready to eat turn upside down to mix in salad dressing.

NUTTY TURMERIC CHICKEN SALAD POT

This deliciously creamy Anglo-Indian chicken salad is reminiscent of the coronation chicken my mum used to make in her coffee shop. Packed with all the health benefits of turmeric and substituting the mayonnaise for coconut milk, this healthy low-carb lunch is a must have on your weekly menu.

Prep Time: 30 minutes | Cook Time: 20 minutes | Servings: 1 | Difficulty: Medium

Gf Ef Sf Gf Df

Ingredients:

For the salad
1 skinless chicken breast
1 tsp. olive oil
30g raisins
86g (1) celery stick, chopped
25g almonds, chopped and roasted (see page 14)
20g sunflower seeds
80g (1/2) avocado
25g (1/4) red onion
25g rocket

For the dressing
1 tsp. ground turmeric
1 tsp. cumin seeds, dry fried and ground
1 tsp. coriander seeds, dry fried and ground
1 tsp. honey
 Fresh basil (1 sprig), finely chopped
4 tbsp. coconut milk
1/2 lime, juice
1 tsp. sesame oil
1 garlic clove, crushed
4g red chilli, sliced thinly
Salt and pepper to taste

Method:

1. Rub 1/2 tsp. olive oil into the chicken breast and season with salt and pepper.
2. Heat the rest of the olive oil in a medium frying pan, add the chicken and cook for approximately 10 minutes on each side until golden brown on the outside and cooked in the middle. Set aside to cool.
3. Combine all salad dressing ingredients in a large mixing bowl and stir thoroughly.
4. Slice the cooked chicken and add to the mixing bowl, along with the raisins, celery, almonds, sunflower seeds, avocado and onion.
5. Stir all ingredients before transferring to jar and topping with rocket.
6. Refrigerate until needed.

COLORFUL CHICKEN SATAY SALAD POT

A vibrant Thai inspired chicken salad. If you like satay chicken, then definitely give this salad a try!

Prep Time: 30 minutes | Cook Time: 20 minutes | Servings: 1 | Difficulty: Medium

Gf Ef Sf Gf Df

Ingredients:

For the dressing
1 tsp. of coconut oil
65g (1) small onion, finely diced
20g (1/8) fresh red chilli, finely chopped
1 clove garlic, crushed
1tsp. coconut sugar
2 tbsp. of peanut butter
6 tbsp. of coconut milk
1 tbsp. tamari sauce
1/2 lime, juice
Salt and pepper to taste

For the salad
1tsp. coconut oil
1 skinless chicken breast
30g (1/4) of red pepper, cut into strips
30g (1/4) avocado, diced
50g (1) carrot, cut into strips
30g mange tout, blanched (see page 14)
20g peanut or cashew nuts, roasted (see page 14)

Method:

1. Heat 1 tsp. of coconut oil in a medium-sized frying pan, season the chicken and add to pan, cook for approximately 10 minutes on each side until golden brown on the outside and cooked in the middle. Set aside to cool.
2. In a small pan, heat 1 tsp. of coconut oil and fry off the onion, garlic and chili until the onion is translucent.
3. Add the coconut sugar and stir until it dissolves.
4. Add in the rest of the dressing ingredients, stir for a couple of minutes, remove from heat and set aside to cool.
5. Add sauce to jar, followed by the sliced chicken, red pepper, avocado, carrot, mange tout and nuts.
6. Refrigerate until needed.
7. When ready to eat turn upside down to mix in salad dressing.

BALSAMIC ROASTED PEACH, CHICKEN AND GOAT'S CHEESE SALAD POT

I love using caramelised peaches in savory dishes. When peaches are grilled the heat intensifies the natural sweetness of the fruit making it a great complement to this lovely chicken salad with its sharp radishes and crunchy green beans.

Prep Time: 30 minutes | Cook Time: 25 minutes | Servings: 1 | Difficulty: Medium

Gf Ef Sf Gf

Ingredients:

For the salad
1 skinless chicken breast
1 tsp. olive oil
1 peach, quartered
30g green beans, blanched (see page 14)
30g radishes, sliced thinly
30g broccoli, blanched (see page 14)
30g (1/4) red onion, chopped thinly
15g almonds, roasted (see page 14) and chopped
40g goats' cheese, sliced

For the dressing
2 tbsp. of olive oil
1 tbsp. balsamic vinegar
1 tsp. honey
Salt and pepper to taste

Method:

1. Preheat oven at 180°C (see table on page 12 for oven conversions).
2. In a large mixing bowl, stir the peaches with the honey and balsamic vinegar until coated.
3. Place them on a baking tray and bake for 20 minutes or until caramelised.
4. Heat 1 tsp. of olive oil in a medium frying pan, season the chicken, add to pan and cook for approximately 10 minutes on each side until golden brown on the outside and cooked in the middle, set aside to cool.
5. Add the dressing ingredients to the bottom of the jar and mix well.
6. Slice the cooked chicken and add to the jar followed by the peaches, green beans, radishes, broccoli and red onion.
7. Top with almonds and goats' cheese.
8. Refrigerate until needed.
9. When ready to eat turn upside down to mix in salad dressing.

CHICKEN AND CASHEW NUT MASSAMAN CURRY POT

This fragrant and hearty curry is a take on a traditional Muslim-style curry from Southern Thailand. Mild and creamy, the heat of the chilli is mellowed out by the addition of the dried spices, coconut milk, onions, potatoes and cashew nuts. A thoroughly tasty and nourishing winter warmer!

Prep Time: 35 minutes | Cook Time: 30 minutes | Servings: 1 | Difficulty: Medium

Gf Ef Sf Gf Df

Ingredients:

For the spice mix
2 tsp. cumin seeds, dry fried and crushed (see page 17)
2 tsp. coriander seeds, dry fried and crushed (see page 17)
1 tsp. mustard seeds, dry fried and crushed (see page 17)
1/4 tsp. ground cayenne pepper
1/4 tsp. ground clove
1/4 tsp. ground cinnamon
1/4 tsp. turmeric
4 cardamom pods (use seeds only)
1 clove of garlic, crushed
4g ginger, grated
4g (1/8) red chilli, finely chopped
2 tbsp. olive oil

For the curry
140g (2) small potatoes, peeled & diced
70g (1/2) onion, diced
1 carrot, peeled and diced
1 tomato, chopped
1 skinless chicken breast, diced
300ml water
125ml coconut milk
1 lime, juice
1 tsp. fish sauce
1 tbsp. tamari sauce
55g cashew nuts, ground
70g (2 florets) broccoli, blanched (see page 14)

Method:

1. Put the potatoes in a medium-sized saucepan with water and boil for about 10-15 minute until potatoes are soft. Drain and set aside.
2. Combine all the spice mix ingredients in a bowl and stir thoroughly.
3. In a large saucepan, fry the onions, tomato and carrots in the spice mixture until the onions are translucent (approximately 3-4 minutes).
4. Add the chicken and fry off for a couple of minutes until coated with the spice mix.
5. Add the water, bring to the boil and simmer for 15 minutes.
6. Add the cooked potatoes, lime juice, coconut milk, tamari sauce and fish sauce and cook for a further 5 minutes or until the chicken is cooked through.
7. Add ground cashew nuts and stir until the curry thickens, then set aside to cool.
8. Once cool, pour curry into jar and top with the blanched broccoli.
9. Refrigerate until needed.
10. Reheat before serving.

MOROCCAN CHICKEN, APRICOT AND ALMOND STEW POT

This tasty chicken dish has vibrant North African flavours. Hearty and healthy, this stew is laced with a sweet combination of spices, honey, almonds and apricots. A delicious belly filling one-pot dish!

Prep Time: 20 minutes | Cook Time: 30 minutes | Servings: 1 | Difficulty: Medium

Gf Ef Sf Gf Df

Ingredients:

1 sweet potato, peeled and diced into small cubes
8g butter
1/2 tsp. cinnamon
1/2 tsp. ginger
1/2 tsp. paprika
1/2 tsp. turmeric
1 clove garlic, crushed
25g (1/4) red onion, diced
1 chicken breast, skinned and diced
118ml water
30g (4) dried apricots, chopped
1 tsp. honey
25g whole almonds, roasted and chopped
80g (1/3) aubergine, diced
75g (1/4) courgette, diced
30g (1/4) red pepper, diced
50g (1/4 of tin) chickpeas
Fresh coriander (1 sprig), finely chopped
Fresh parsley (1 sprig), finely chopped
Salt and pepper

Method:

1. In a saucepan of boiling water cook the sweet potato for approximately 10 minute or until cooked. Drain and set aside.
2. Heat a casserole dish over a medium-to-low heat and add the butter, cinnamon, ginger, paprika, turmeric, garlic, red onion and fry for 3-4 minutes until the onion is translucent.
3. Season the chicken, add to spice mix and fry for a couple more minutes until lightly colored and well-coated, stirring frequently.
4. Add the water, apricots, honey, almonds, aubergine, courgette and red pepper, bring to the boil, reduce heat and simmer for approximately 20-25 minutes until chicken is cooked and sauce has thickened.
5. Add chickpeas, sweet potato, coriander and parsley, and stir for a couple more minutes before removing from heat. Cool and transfer to jar.
6. Refrigerate until needed.
7. Reheat before serving.

LEBANESE CHICKEN SALAD POT

This Middle Eastern inspired dish has a light, refreshing, zesty kick to it. The tangy Greek yogurt, herb and spice mix dressing transforms the simple salad ingredients and keeps the chicken moist and succulent.

Prep Time: 30 minutes | Cook Time: 20 minutes | Servings: 1 serving | Difficulty: Medium

Gf Ef Sf Gf Nf

Ingredients:

For the salad
1 tsp. olive oil
1 skinless chicken breast
60g (6) cherry tomatoes, quarters
65g (1/5) cucumber, seeded and diced
30g (1/4) avocado
35g (1/4) yellow pepper, diced
35g (1/4) green pepper, diced
30g (1/2) red onion, diced
20g rocket

Yoghurt dressing
Fresh thyme (3 sprigs), leaves pulled off, chopped finely
1 tbsp. sesame seeds, dry fried and ground (see page 17)
1 tbsp. cumin seeds, dry fried and ground (see page 17)
1/4 tsp. cayenne pepper
1 tsp. dried oregano
1 clove of garlic, crushed
Fresh mint (2 sprigs), chopped finely
1/2 tsp. sea salt
1/2 tsp. ground back peppercorn
5 tbsp. (75g) Greek yoghurt
1/2 tsp. paprika
1/2 lemon, zest and juice

Method:

1. Heat 1 tsp. olive oil in a frying pan, season the chicken and fry for approximately 10 minutes on each side until golden brown on the outside and cooked in the middle. Set aside to cool.
2. In a pestle and mortar add the fresh thyme, sesame seeds, cumin seeds, cayenne pepper, oregano, garlic, mint, salt and black pepper and grind together.
3. In a medium-sized bowl combine the herb mix, Greek yogurt, paprika, and lemon zest and juice. Mix well.
4. Dice the chicken and mix with the yogurt dressing. Transfer to jar.
5. Add the cherry tomatoes, cucumber, yellow and green pepper and onion.
6. Top with rocket.
7. Refrigerate until needed.

CHAPTER 5
Meat Lunch Pots

DUCK, BLUEBERRY AND BASIL SALAD POT

Growing up in the Périgord region of France where duck is on almost every menu, it has always been one of my favourite meats. It partners well with fruit, so the blueberry and basil dressing adds the perfect finishing touches to this salad.

Prep Time: 35 minutes | Cook Time: 25 minutes | Servings: 1 | Difficulty: Medium

Gf Ef Sf Gf Df

Ingredients:

For the Salad
1 duck breast
1/2 red pepper, sliced
1/4 avocado, diced
80g (1) carrots, peeled, cut into thirds and sliced long ways
50g blueberries
40g goats' cheese
25g of walnuts roasted (see page 14)
25g red lettuce, shredded (can be substituted for baby spinach)

For the dressing
1 tbsp. blueberry jam
2 tbsp. of cold pressed olive oil
1 tbsp. of apple cider vinegar
1/2 lemon, zest and juice
1 tsp. Dijon mustard
Fresh basil (8 leaves), finely chopped
1/4 tsp. ground black peppercorns
Salt to taste

Method:

1. Cook the duck breast following the instructions below.
2. Add all dressing ingredients to the bottom of the jar and mix well to combine.
3. Once the duck has cooled, slice and add to the jar.
4. Add the red pepper, avocado, carrots and blueberries to the jar.
5. Top with the walnuts, goats' cheese and red lettuce or baby spinach.

Cooking Duck

1. Preheat oven to 220°C (see table on page 12 for oven conversions)
2. Score the skin of the duck breast diagonally 4 or 5 times and sprinkle with salt and pepper.
3. Place skin side down in a cold non stick frying pan on a medium heat without oil for 6-8 minutes or until golden brown (pour fat off regularly).
4. Cook on other side for 60 seconds.
5. Place on a rack in the oven skin side down for 10-18 minutes depending on cooking preference.
6. Set aside for 10 minutes to cool while you prepare the rest of the salad.

THAI BEEF SALAD POT

The Thai style dressing for this salad acts as a great in-the-jar marinade for the steak saving you lots of preparation time. Leave overnight for best results. A great refreshing summer salad!

Prep Time: 20 minutes | Cook Time: 6 minutes | Servings: 1 | Difficulty: Medium

Gf Ef Sf Gf Df

Ingredients:

For the dressing
2 tbsp. sesame oil
1 tbsp. + 1tsp. tamari sauce
1/2 tsp. fish sauce
1 tsp. of coconut sugar
1/2 lime, zest and juice
Fresh mint (8 leaves) chopped finely
Fresh basil (8 leaves) chopped finely
Fresh coriander (8 leaves) chopped finely
4g of red chilli, sliced thinly
1 garlic clove, crushed
4g of ginger, grated

For the salad
1 tsp. of coconut oil
1 sirloin or rib eye steak
1 (70g) carrot, peeled and cut into strips
50g 5 baby plum tomatoes, quartered
35g (1/3) red pepper, sliced
35g (1/8) cucumber, seeded and cut into strips
1/4 red onion, chopped
20g cashew nuts roasted (see page 14)
20g baby spinach

Method:

1. Heat the coconut oil in a frying pan, season the steak and fry for about 2 to 3 minutes on each side for medium rare (vary the cooking time based on personal preference and the thickness of steak).
2. Once cooked. Set aside to cool.
3. Combine all the dressing ingredients in the bottom of the jar and mix well.
4. Slice the steak and add to jar. Follow with the carrot, cucumber, baby tomatoes and red pepper.
5. Top with baby spinach and roasted cashew nuts.
6. Refrigerate until needed.
7. When ready to eat turn upside down to mix in salad dressing.

BACON AND EGG SALAD POT WITH OVEN ROASTED ASPARAGUS AND BUTTON MUSHROOMS

My dad's favourite bacon and eggs has been the inspiration behind this dish. I wanted to see if I could take a British favourite and turn it into a healthy lunchtime salad.

Prep Time: 25 minutes | Cook Time: 15 minutes | Servings: 1 | Difficulty: Medium

Gf Sf Gf Df Nf

Ingredients:

For the dressing
2 tbsp. olive oil
1 tbsp. apple cider vinegar
1 tsp. wholegrain mustard
1/4 lemon, juice
Fresh parsley (2 sprigs) chopped finely
1 clove of garlic, minced
Salt and pepper

For the roasted vegetables and bacon
55g (6) button mushroom, sliced in half
50g (6) asparagus, ends removed and cut into thirds
1 tbsp. butter, cut into pieces
2 cloves of garlic, minced
Salt and pepper
2/3 rashers of bacon, cut in half

For the salad
1 medium egg
65g of green beans, blanched (see page 13), cut into thirds
40g (5) cherry tomatoes, chopped in half

Method:

1. Pre-heat oven to 220C° (see table on page 12 for oven conversions)
3. In a large baking tray, place the button mushrooms and asparagus to one side, topped with the butter, garlic and salt and pepper and place the rashers of bacon on the other side. Bake for approximately 15 minutes until cooked turning over occasionally. Once cooked set aside to cool.
4. Place the egg in a saucepan, cover with water, bring to the boil and simmer for 6-8 minutes for a boiled egg (you may vary the timing based on personal preference). Once cooked, run under cold water, peel and cut in half.
Combine all the salad dressing ingredients in the bottom of the jar and mix well.
5. Layer the jar with the mushrooms and asparagus first, followed by the green beans, cherry tomatoes, and then the bacon and egg.
6. Refrigerate until needed.
7. When ready to eat turn upside down to mix in salad dressing.

Notes: To remove the woody ends of asparagus snap off the lower part of the stem. It will naturally snap where it starts to get tough.

MIXED PEA, MINT, FETA AND BACON SALAD POT

Peas and mint are a classic combination. Combined with the roasted sweet potato and bacon, this salad makes for a tasty and refreshing summer lunch.

Prep Time: 20 minutes | Cook Time: 30 minutes | Servings: 1 | Difficulty: Medium

Gf Ef Sf Gf Nf

Ingredients:

For the sweet potato
260g sweet potato, peeled and diced into small cubes
1 tbsp. olive oil
1 tsp. honey
Salt and pepper
2/3 rashers of bacon, cut in half

For the dressing
2 tbsp. olive oil
1 tbsp. apple cider vinegar
1/2 lemon juice
1 tsp. honey
Fresh mint (25 leaves), finely chopped
1 clove of garlic, crushed
Salt and pepper

For The Salad
50g garden peas (frozen) blanched (see page 14)
50g mange tout blanched (see page 14) and halved
65g feta diced

Method:

1. Pre-heat oven at 180C° (see table on page 12 for oven conversions)
2. In a baking tray mix the sweet potato with the honey, olive oil and salt and pepper.
3. Bake for approximately 30 minutes or until crisp, turning occasionally. After the first 15 minutes place the bacon rashers on the other side of the baking tray, turning once (bake for 15 minutes). Set aside to cool.
4. Combine dressing ingredients in the bottom of the jar and mix well.
5. Add the peas and mange tout to jar, followed by the sweet potato, feta and bacon.
6. Refrigerate until needed.
7. When ready to eat turn upside down to mix in salad dressing.

Conclusion

I hope this book has helped you to get creative in the kitchen and has inspired you to include more delicious fruit and vegetables in your diet.

For further nutritional tips and advice to help you become a happier and healthier version of yourself, please visit:

www.earthinspired.co.uk

May you succeed in making beautiful, delicious, nourishing lunches!

All the best!

Fiona Manning

www.earthinspired.co.uk

Index

A
Almonds, 14, 34, 38, 41, 43, 45
Apple Cider Vinegar, 22, 36-37, 48, 50-51
Apricots
    Dried, 45
Asparagus, 50
Aubergine, 15, 45
Avocado, 19, 21-22, 25-29, 34, 36, 38, 40-42, 46, 48

B
Baby spinach, 48-49
Bacon, 50-51
Balsamic Vinegar, 19-21, 26, 28, 43
Basil, 25-26, 29, 36, 41, 48-49
Beef
    Rib eye steak, 49
    Sirloin steak, 49
Beetroot, 16, 21, 23
Blanched Vegetables, 14
Bluberries
    Jam, 48
Blue Cheese, 19
Broccoli, 10, 14, 31-32, 34, 43-44
Butter, 22, 45, 50
Butter beans, 37
Button Mushrooms, 50

C
Cannellini beans, 27
Capers, 29, 35, 37
Cardamom Pods, 44
Carrot, 23-25, 30-31, 36, 42, 44, 48-49
Cashew Nuts, 14, 24-25, 30-31, 36, 40, 42, 44, 49
Cayenne Pepper, 15, 20, 27, 30-31, 44, 46
Celery, 38, 41
Chicken
    Balsamic roasted peach and goat's cheese, 43
    Lebanese, 46
    Massaman curry, 44
    Morrocan, apricot and almond, 45
    Nutty turmeric, 41
    Satay, 42
    Spicy mango and grape, 40
Chickpea, 30, 32, 45
Chilli, 24-25, 27, 31-32, 36, 38, 40-42, 44, 49
Chive, 22
Cinnamon
    Ground, 30, 32, 38, 44-45
Clove
    Ground, 31-32, 44
Coconut Milk, 31-32, 38, 41-42, 44
Coconut oil, 42, 49
Coconut Sugar, 11, 27, 42, 49
Cooking Duck, 48
Coriander
    Fresh , 24-25, 36, 40, 45, 49
    Seeds, 17, 30-32, 38, 41, 44
Courgette, 15-16, 20, 23, 25, 30-31, 45
Cucumber, 29, 35, 40, 46, 49
Cumin Seeds, 15, 17, 20, 30-32, 38, 41, 44, 46
Curley kale, 14, 24
Curry, 10, 31-32, 38, 44

D
Dairy free, 24-25, 27, 31-32, 34-38, 40-42, 44-45, 48-50
Dressing
    Ginger peanut dressing, 24
    Lemon butter dressing, 22
    Yoghurt dressing, 46
Duck
    Blueberry and basil, 48

E
Egg free, 19-32, 34-38, 40-46, 48-49
Endive, 34

F
Feta, 14-15, 23, 26, 29-30, 51
Fish sauce, 36, 44, 49

G
Garlic
    Clove, 24, 27, 31-32, 35, 37-38, 40-42, 44-46, 49-51

Ginger
    Fresh, 24-25, 40, 49

M
Mange Tout, 14, 19, 32, 36, 42, 51
Mango, 25, 40
Maple syrup, 15, 20, 36
Mint, 25, 30, 46, 49, 51
Mushrooms
    Button, 50
Mustard
    Dijon, 29, 48
    Seeds, 17, 44
    Wholegrain, 35, 50

N
Nut free, 22, 27, 29, 37, 46, 50-51

O
Olives
    Black, 26, 29
    Green, 26, 29
Onion
Ground, 30, 32, 36, 44-45
Gluten free, 19-32, 34-38, 40-46, 48-51
Goat's Cheese, 15-16, 20-21, 28, 43, 48
Grain free, 19-32, 34-38, 40-46, 48-51
Grapes, 28, 38, 40
Greek Yoghurt, 46
Green beans, 14, 21, 35, 37, 43, 50
Grinding Seeds, 17

H
Hazelnut, 14-15, 19
Honey, 11, 16, 21, 24-26, 28, 30, 38, 40-41, 43, 45, 51

K
Key Measurements, 12
Kidney beans, 27

L
Layering A Jar, 10
Lemon, 22, 27, 29, 35, 37, 46, 48, 50-51
Lemon grass, 36
Lime, 25, 27, 31-32, 36, 40-42, 44, 49
    Red, 26-29, 37, 40-41, 43, 45-46, 49
    Spring, 35
    White, 22, 31-32, 42, 44
    Orange, 34
Oregano
    Dried, 29, 46
Oven Temperature Conversions, 12

P
Paprika, 45-46
Parsley, 45, 50
Parsnip, 23, 30
Peach, 43
Peanut Butter, 24, 42
Peanuts, 42
Pear, 19
Peas
    Frozen, 14, 22, 51
Peppercorns
Black, 34-35, 46, 48
Peppers
    Green, 27, 30, 46
    Red, 15, 19-27, 29-30, 32, 34-37, 40, 42, 45, 48-49
    Yellow, 26, 29, 46
    Pine Nut, 15, 23, 26, 34
Potatoes
    Red, 22
    Sweet, 23, 30, 32, 45, 51
    Pumpkin, 15, 20

R
Radishes, 19, 21, 36-37, 43
Raisins, 41
Red Cabbage, 24
Red Lentil, 31
Red lettuce, 48
Red Wine Vinegar, 27, 29, 35
Roasted Nuts, 14, 16
Rocket, 19, 26, 28, 35, 41, 46

S
Salmon
- Curry spiced with celery and grape, 38
- Orange and thyme and endive, 34
- Thai spiced, 36

Seared Tuna Steak, 35

Sesame oil
- Toasted, 40

Soya free, 19-32, 34-38, 40-46, 48-51
Sunflower seeds, 41
Sweet Corn, 10, 27, 35
Sweet Potato, 23, 30, 32, 45, 51

T
Tamari Sauce, 11, 24-25, 31-32, 36, 38, 40, 42, 44, 49

Tarragon
- Dried, 22, 37

Thyme
- Fresh, 34, 36

Tomatoes
- Baby plum, 49
- Cherry, 22, 27, 29, 34, 37, 46, 50
- Paste, 31
- Sun-dried, 22, 35

Tuna, 35, 37

Turmeric
- Ground, 31-32, 38, 41, 44-45

V
Vegan, 27, 31-32
Vegetarian, 10-11, 19-33

W
Walnut, 14-15, 20-21, 28, 35, 48

Printed by Amazon Italia Logistica S.r.l.
Torrazza Piemonte (TO), Italy